Waking Up Just In Time

Waking Up Just In Time

A therapist shows how to use the *Twelve Steps* approach to life's ups and downs

ABRAHAM J. TWERSKI, M.D.

PEANUTS® cartoons by Charles M. Schulz

TOPPER BOOKS

AN IMPRINT OF PHAROS BOOKS • A SCRIPPS HOWARD COMPANY

NEW YORK

Text copyright© 1990 by Abraham J. Twerski

PEANUTS® Comic Strips: © 1953 through 1990 United Feature
Syndicate, Inc.

The Twelve Steps are reprinted with permission of Alcoholics
Anonymous World Services, Inc. Adaptations of this material are found
throughout the book.

First published in 1990.
Library of Congress Cataloging-in-Publication Data
Twerski, Abraham J.
    Waking up just in time: a therapist shows how to use the twelve-steps
approach to life's ups and downs/ Abraham J. Twerski;
Peanuts cartoons by Charles M. Schulz.
    p.cm.
    ISBN 0-88687-472-6 : $6.95
    1. Conduct of life. 2. Problem solving. I. Schulz, Charles M. II.
Title. III. Title: Twelve-steps approach to life's ups and downs.
BF698. T85 1990
158'.1--dc20

Pharos ISBN: 0-88687-472-6

Printed in United States of America
TOPPER BOOKS
An Imprint of Pharos Books
A Scripps Howard Company
200 Park Avenue
New York, NY 10166

10   9   8   7   6   5   4   3   2   1

Contents

Steps and Slogans

In the classroom, Marcie's answer was right and Peppermint Patty's answer was wrong. In real life, both are right.

The answer to most of life's problems does lie within the heart of all mankind. The reason so many people experience distress and encounter so many difficulties in life is that they are unaware that the answers to most of their problems lie right within them. Peppermint Patty is right.

And so is Marcie. Many people have found twelve steps they can take that can help them adjust to life in such a way that many thorny problems can be resolved. These twelve steps show us how to use the resources within ourselves to adapt to life and how to enlist the help of a higher power when our own resources are inadequate.

A number of years ago, I encountered a problem all too familiar to many people. I sat down at the checkbook to pay the monthly bills, only to discover to my distress that there was no money in the checking account.

Since we had not had any unusual expenditures, I could not understand how this had happened. But since figures do not lie, I had no option other than to delay payment of my bills until the following month.

For two weeks I was quite irritable and very upset with myself for having somehow gotten myself into this predicament. At the beginning of the next month the bank statement arrived, and to my very pleasant surprise I discovered that I *did* have money in my account. What had happened was simply that I was on direct deposit, and when my paycheck was deposited directly to my account I had forgotten one time to record the deposit in the checkbook.

Did I need a loan? No. Did I need charity? Of course not. I simply needed to be made aware of the true state of affairs.

I did have the money, but since I did not know I had it, I could not use it.

So many people have more than adequate personality strengths and resources to cope effectively with most of life's challenges. The reason we often fail to cope is not that we lack the capacity to do so but that we are *unaware* that we have such capabilities. Our anxiety and distress is thus totally unwarranted.

If the question is "Where does one find the capabilities of coping effectively with life?," then Peppermint Party is completely right. The resources are within ourselves. If the question is "How can we discover these resources?," then Marcie is right. The answer is twelve, the twelve steps that help us discover our own strengths and show us where to turn for additional help.

The Twelve Steps to Everywhere

Back in the 1930s, two men whose lives had been decimated by their drinking and who were patently helpless to stop their self- destructive behavior devised a method of recovery based on mutual help.

Out of this modest beginning emerged the fellowship of Alcoholics Anonymous, which now has thousands of groups across the globe and millions of participants.

The success of this program led to its emulation by persons with problems other than alcoholism who were unable to overcome their problems by traditional modes of treatment.

We now have Narcotics Anonymous, Overeaters Anonymous, Gamblers Anonymous, Pills Anonymous, Debtors Anonymous, Cocaine Anonymous, Emotions Anonymous, Sex and Love Anonymous, Families Anonymous, and others. Many of these have complementary groups for significant others, such as Al-Anon, Nar-Anon, Gam-Anon, or Adult Children of Alcoholics.

These fellowships have indeed produced remarkable results in many cases that have defied the finest psychiatric and psychological treatments.

It is only logical to try to understand just what makes these programs so effective and then apply these principles to other problems of living that so often appear insoluble.

The common denominator of these programs is an agenda of twelve steps that has been adapted for various self-defeating behaviors. The modus operandi of these programs is the mutual sharing of difficulties and of success, which is accomplished by the medium of meetings wherein people share their experience, hope, strength, and courage.

In addition to benefiting from the collective wisdom of the group, each member is expected to have a personal sponsor or mentor. Common terminology that has special meaning to the initiated is employed, and there is a lexicon of pithy slogans.

Although the programs do not espouse any specific religion, prayer is an important feature.

The Twelve Steps Are:

1. We admitted we were powerless (over alcohol, narcotics, food, gambling, and so on) that our lives had become unmanageable.
2. We came to believe that a power greater than ourselves could restore us to sanity.
3. We made a decision to turn our will and our lives over to the care of God as we understood Him.
4. We made a searching and fearless moral inventory of ourselves.
5. We admitted to God, to ourselves, and to another human being the exact nature of our wrongs.
6. We were entirely ready to have God remove all these defects of character.
7. We humbly asked Him to remove our shortcomings.
8. We made a list of all persons we had harmed, and became willing to make amends to them all.
9. We made direct amends to such people wherever possible, except when to do so would injure them or others.
10. We continued to take personal inventory and when we were wrong promptly admitted it.
11. We sought through prayer and meditation to improve our conscious contact with God as we understood Him, praying only for knowledge of His will for us and the power to carry that out.
12. Having had a spiritual awakening as the result of these steps, we tried to carry the message (to alcoholics, drug addicts, gamblers, food addicts, and the like) and to practice these principles in all our affairs.

Some of the More Commonly Employed Slogans Are:

Time Takes Time

Easy Does It

Live and Let Live

One Day at a Time

Keep It Simple

Keep Coming Back, It Works!

Let Go and Let God

First Things First

Think, Think, Think

The most widely used prayer is the Serenity Prayer:

God, grant me the serenity to accept the things I cannot change, the courage to change the things I can, and the wisdom to know the difference.

The entire program is geared to help an individual correct misperceptions of reality, to make an optimum adjustment to reality, to achieve an accurate self-appraisal, to rid oneself of character flaws, and to help others who have similar problems.

The problems of living are certainly not unique to people who have an addiction problem. We are all beset with problems of one type or another, and in our desperation to resolve them we often resort to counterproductive behavior and attitudes.

We might profit by exploiting some of the techniques that have proved so beneficial and successful in overcoming some of the most obstinate self-destructive behaviors known. Why not look at some of the more common problems of living and see how application of the principles of the twelve-step program might be helpful in their resolution?

A number of years ago, while engaged in training psychiatric residents, I found that I could convey some psychological concepts more rapidly and more effectively by using the insightful cartoon strips created by Charles Schulz. This led to the publication of a book, *When Do the Good Things Start?*

I would now like to return to that virtually inexhaustible well of psychology and use the actions and interactions of the *Peanuts* comic-strip characters to demonstrate some of the more common problems of human behavior, and suggest how they may be mitigated or remedied by the approach utilized in the twelve-step program.

1

We Admitted We Were Powerless ... That Our Lives Had Become Unmanageable

When a person consults a psychiatrist or psychologist about a problem, he has already taken a major step toward its solution: he has recognized that there is a problem and has admitted that he needs help. At least in one area of his life, something has obviously become *unmanageable*. Obviously? Of course! If it were not *un-manageable*, then it would be manageable. If it were manageable, why would he be seeking help?

It is often difficult for people to describe their state of affairs so explicitly. Many people have difficulty admitting to themselves, let alone to someone else, that any part of their lives has become un-manageable. We tend to think—perhaps because we like to think— that we are in control of everything. Even when we seek help with a given problem, we may still hang on to the notion that we are in full control. This is, of course, a patent contradiction, and it may stand in the way of accepting the help that is being offered.

For a long time I did not realize why some patients who came for help with a particular problem rejected my recommendations and

continued on a downhill road, doing more of what had been unsuc-
cessful in the past. Eventually I realized that they were in deep conflict. On the one hand, something had become unmanageable, and
on the other hand, they could not admit it.

Sometimes people do not go for help when a problem is unmanageable, but instead divert their attention and make believe that the
problem does not exist. They get involved with other things and
hope that the problem will somehow correct itself. Sometimes this
indeed happens. But too often the problem just stays where it is or
(more frequently) gets worse.

People may escape from a problem into drinking or using some
kind of mind-altering substance. Or they may escape into gambling,
overeating, or sex. These escapes may provide a temporary sense of
relief, but the problem remains unsolved.

Often, more than just one area of life becomes unmanageable.
Our whole lives can become unmanageable, and we may do some
very destructive things as a result. If we fail to take proper action,

the true state of our circumstances eventually becomes evident; yet, instead of finding some constructive solution we may turn to one of the escape routes and the damage we have done to ourselves or others remains unrepaired.

Linus would undoubtedly like to think of himself as an expert paddleball player. In fact, he is a very poor one. His persistence at doing something at which he is not at all proficient gets him into trouble. Furniture is upset, lamps are turned over, and vases are broken.

What does Linus do? He is obviously angry at the world for having allowed such terrible things to happen. But instead of trying to set things straight, Linus resorts to the comfort of his thumb and security blanket, leaving behind the destruction that resulted from his behavior.

What Makes Life Unmanageable?

Most often it is a failure to perceive reality correctly. If an electric wire is "live" but one handles it as though it were "dead," one will get into much trouble quickly. A person who is barely earning a living wage but spends money as though he were a multimillionaire will soon be in great difficulty. It stands to reason that if one misperceives reality, life will become unmanageable.

It is amazing how often people misperceive reality. Most of what brings people to the attention of a psychiatrist or psychologist is a misperception of reality. In the case of the psychotic, the misperceptions are gross—delusions or hallucinations. In other cases, they are much more subtle but no less destructive.

For example, people who cannot accept the reality of a loss, a failure, or a disappointment tend to get into difficulties. When unpleasant things that are unchangeable happen, the only reasonable approach is to accept them and go on with life. If one tries to deny the reality, whether by drinking, sedating oneself with drugs, overeating, or fleeing into some other preoccupation, the results will not be good. Escaping reality does not change reality in the least, yet we often delude ourselves that we have overcome the problem by one or more escapist techniques.

Snoopy is brokenhearted over a failed romance. Charlie Brown's suggestion to forget it would be sound advice if this were to mean "Put it behind you and get on with your life." Snoopy, however, understands it to mean that he should find some way to forget, and then and only then can life proceed.

Snoopy does not use alcohol or drugs but does escape into food, as many humans do. When the relief provided by eating gives only fleeting comfort, Snoopy continues eating.

Snoopy becomes convinced that his method is working. "I've done it! I've forgotten her!" He fails to see the contradiction that if you *know* you've forgotten, you are actually remembering.

Snoopy's indulgence in food has done nothing to solve his problem. All he has accomplished is growing obese and deluding himself that he has overcome his problem.

Food, gambling, alcohol, drugs, work, sex—whatever. When anything is done to excess in an effort to blot out reality, the results are always negative.

If you don't like what has happened and can't change it, put the past behind you and go on with life. That's the only constructive adjustment to reality.

The obvious is not always obvious. Some people get into difficulties because of destructive behavior patterns such as laziness, and although they know that they are in trouble, they are simply unable to see the obvious. For example, the person who gets up late every morning and dillydallys around until way past noon may wonder why he never seems to get anything accomplished.

These kinds of behavior patterns make our lives, or at least some segments thereof, completely unmanageable. Why don't we do something about it? Simply because we don't admit the true nature of the problem. We may not get our day started until others are halfway through theirs, but we cannot correct the problem because we don't admit to ourselves what the problem is. We are lazy, but we just won't admit it.

You can tell Charlie the obvious. As long as he chooses the easier way and watches television instead of doing his assignment, he will never get anything accomplished. But Charlie simply is unable to recognize this. He sits in front of the TV wondering what's wrong. If you had the opportunity, perhaps you would like to enlighten

Charlie as to why he never gets anything done. Of course, perhaps right at this moment, there is someone who is trying to enlighten you. You might be able to correct some faulty behavior of your own if only you recognized it.

Why not ask some reliable person for an objective opinion?

The refusal to recognize that things have gotten out of control is called *denial*. Denial is not the same as lying, because in denial the person actually believes his own distortion of reality.

Our minds are very clever in producing denial. For example, we may have the very same trait we condemn in others, but we make it more acceptable by giving it another name:

I am very firm in my opinion. *You* are obstinate.
I am very deliberate in my actions and give things serious thought before doing them. *You* are a hopeless procrastinator.
I am very witty. *You* are a buffoon.

This would be a cute little game if the consequences were not so serious. I have heard the remark "My husband is not an alcoholic, but I do think he drinks more than he should." Or "I know that my daughter binges every so often, then goes on a starvation diet to keep her weight down, but she is not really bulemic."

Here is a good rule of thumb: If something *causes* a problem, it *is*

a problem. Making believe that it is not will only allow the problem to continue.

What is rationalization? Rationalization is making up good reasons instead of admitting the true reasons. Rationalization is so common that if we were to stop rationalizing, the silence would be intolerable.

Not only do we rationalize when we speak to other people and give them logical reasons for why we did or did not do something, but much rationalization also goes on silently, internally. Often we are not aware that we are rationalizing.

We rationalize to cover up something. If we are unable to admit to something, we give a plausible reason that makes it unnecessary for us to face the truth.

Failure to recognize the truth precludes taking the necessary steps that would correct a problem. In order to take any kind of corrective action, one must first accept that some kind of problem exists—or, in other words, that something has become *unmanageable*.

Lucy cannot field well. Lucy *never* catches the ball whether it is a pop fly or a grounder, but Lucy never admits her deficiency in fielding. Lucy always has an excuse. Lucy's fielding will never improve until she recognizes that her fielding is unmanageable.

Sometimes our lives, or some aspect of our lives, become unmanageable, yet we may be obstinate in refusing to make any changes. We may perservere in self-defeating behavior.

People often refer to such a behavior pattern as "being afraid of success." Why would anyone be afraid of success? Isn't it natural to prefer success over failure?

The answer is that as unpleasant as failure may be, it has one redeeming feature. Failure often terminates responsibility, whereas success tends to generate new responsibility. If you fail at a task, no one is likely to make more demands on you, and even your own expectations of yourself diminish. If you succeed, you may well be expected to continue to perform.

Getting on base raises problems. You have to decide whether to advance yourself and, should you reach second base, you may have to try for third and even home. All this can be avoided simply by striking out and getting the whole ordeal over with.

*T*ension is part of normal life. Sorry, folks, but that's a fact. Our choice is not whether or not we can avoid tension, because tension is unavoidable. Our only choice is how we *manage* tension.

What constitutes tension? This is highly variable. For one person, tension exists when he has to make a life-or-death decision. For

another person, deciding what tie or dress to wear can produce unbearable tension.

There are only two approaches to tension: (1) to cope effectively with the situation that is producing it or (2) to escape the problem one way or another. Some people try to escape by drinking or taking pills or drugs. Others try to eat their way out. A bit of clear thinking would reveal the obvious: Escaping never solves the problem.

Waiting to see on which side of the net the ball will fall is too tense a condition for Snoopy to tolerate. Snoopy's solution is to take another chocolate chip cookie.

How does eating solve the situation? It doesn't. In fact, the tension continues and becomes more difficult to tolerate. Snoopy may well need another cookie to deal with the additional tension, and another, and another . . .

One of the characteristics of unmanageability is contained in the motto "If at first you don't succeed, quit!"

If you fail at something, you have the option of either "try and try again" or "quit."

For some people, failure has become a way of life. They are quite familiar with failure. Hence it is actually a more desirable result than success. Success is an unknown, and the unknown can be frightening.

Recidivist criminals often reject rehabilitative efforts because, with all its drawbacks, prison life is at least familiar. Children who run away from abusive parents return to certain punishment because the known, as painful as it might be, is more tolerable than the unknown.

Poor Charlie Brown. He seems to be unable to succeed at anything. His solution: adapt to a philosophy of failure. Become fascinated with failure. It's going to happen anyway, so try to enjoy it.

If we only recognized our strengths, admitted our shortcomings, and made the necessary adaptations that would likely result in success, we could indeed succeed. It just might be a bit harder than resigning oneself to failure.

2

We Came to Believe That a Power Greater Than Ourselves Could Restore Us to Sanity

Step two is the only logical conclusion that can follow step one.

If I am powerless over some aspect of my life and if there is to be a change, then obviously I am not the one capable of making that change by myself. If I could, I would not be powerless and my life would not be unmanageable.

I often wonder why some people have so much difficulty with step two. After all, if they have a problem with the plumbing that is more complicated than replacing a washer in the faucet, they have no difficulty in calling a plumber. We resort to a power greater than ourselves many times during a typical day, so why is there so much resistance to asking for help from a power greater than our own with any of life's problems, whatever they may be?

Perhaps the answer is that whereas we do not expect ourselves to be experts in plumbing, electricity, or any other particular technical area, we do expect ourselves to be expert in managing *all* aspects of our lives. But what if some aspects of our lives somehow or other get out of control? What is wrong with recognizing this and looking for a source outside ourselves for help?

Sometimes we actually do so when we enlist the help of a psychiatrist, psychologist, or other counselor. But what if their help doesn't work? Then we must look elsewhere for a Higher Power.

If you don't wish to capitalize *higher power*, you may think of it as being a self-help group. If you are more religiously inclined, then the higher power can be God.

Some people claim they don't believe there is a God. Often this is not quite accurate, because they *do* believe there is a God. The trouble is that they think *they* are He.

As long as we hold on to our ideas of our own omnipotence, we are essentially thinking of ourselves as God, and of course we cannot then believe in a supreme being, because there cannot be *two* Gods. After we take step one sincerely and admit that we are not omnipotent and that we are not God, it becomes relatively easy to think of God as the higher power.

So reflect a bit on step one. If you have taken it seriously, the climb to step two is a very small one indeed.

It is difficult to accept that there is a power greater than oneself when one believes oneself to be the greatest.

We tend to think of humility as a virtue, a trait that is essential if one aspires to piety or high ideals. Actually, humility is essential for day-to-day living. If we don't admit our limitations, then we may try to be our own doctors, our own lawyers, our own electricians, our own tax accountants—and we can get into a great deal of trouble fast.

Since we probably admit that we are not universal geniuses, evidenced by the fact that we do enlist the help of doctors or automobile mechanics, why must we insist that we have infinite wisdom in all other aspects of life, especially in our personal lives, when it be-

comes evident that some aspects of our lives have become unmanageable?

A bit of humility will allow us to look outside ourselves for much-needed help.

One alcoholic described how he desperately tried to get control over his life for years and finally came to the conclusion that only some greater force could set him straight. He began to search for God but could not find Him in any of the places God is usually thought to reside.

One day he was walking along the seashore, totally dejected, having been evicted from his home. "I looked up at the sky and shouted, 'If You are up there, then help me!' And, you know, He did help me. I am now six years sober."

We do not have to be specific. We do not even have to know what we need. All we need to do is recognize that we need help and ask for it.

Some people consider religion a cop-out. They say that expecting God to do things for you is nothing but laziness, pushing onto God something you should be doing by yourself.

This is a gross misunderstanding of religion. We are expected to do whatever is within our capacity. Religion does not advocate sitting in the passenger seat and asking God to do the driving, but sitting behind the wheel, driving safely and cautiously, and praying to God to protect you from some other guy who may not be driving safely or from any other danger beyond your control.

It is not being lazy to pray for help with something that is *beyond* your own capacity. What else can you do about something that is beyond your capacity? Worry about it? How is that going to help?

If your roof is leaking, you can do something about it: Get it repaired! If it is raining cats and dogs and you have failed to waterproof your basement, relying instead on God's promise to Noah, you are rather foolish. God never promised not to flood your basement.

But if you're worried that the whole world is going under, just what do you plan on doing about that? Where do you plan to take refuge?

If you conclude that you are indeed powerless over something, it is really insanity to continue to try to exert control over it. That's where step two takes a load off your mind and allows you to utilize your energies for those things you *can* do something about.

There are many houses of worship: churches, temples, mosques, and the like. Many people flock into these buildings, yet many emerge much the same as they entered.

A house of worship is really a place of learning. One should be seeking guidelines on how to live properly, how to do what is right, and how to know what is right.

Trying to learn what is right is absolutely impossible if one believes that one *already knows* what is right. If we recognize our own limitations and fallibility, we can sincerely look to be taught and guided.

Snoopy's title really is perfect. Theology is based on the premise that the human mind is limited, fallible, and vulnerable to pressures and desires that distort our perception and our thinking.

If being in a house of worship doesn't affect a person's behavior, it is probably because that person went in to tell God what He should do, having come to the conclusion that one knows what is best for Him. If one goes in with an open mind, considering that one might be wrong, and asks for divine guidance, one might come out with the right answers.

If we must be restored to sanity, then what we are doing now must be *in*sane. Are we really doing things that are crazy?

Look at it this way. If what we are doing is really and truly what we want to do, then doing so makes perfectly good sense. If what we are doing is *not* what we want to do, but we have to do it because someone is pointing a gun at our heads, doing so also makes perfectly good sense. But if we find ourselves doing something we really do not want to do and nobody is forcing us to do it, then doing it makes no sense at all. And if we are doing something nonsensical, isn't that really "insane"?

If you find your willpower is being overridden and you do things you don't want to do, you need a higher power to help you stop doing nonsensical things. *That* is being restored to sanity.

3

We Made A Decision To Turn Our Will And Our Lives Over To The Care Of God As We Understood Him.

*T*here is a pitfall in step three. Allowing yourself total freedom in conceptualizing God can result in some rather strange ideas about religion.

In many religions there are both fundamentals and trimmings. Just as a house is not really complete without some of the decorative components such as paint and wallpaper, neither is religion fully complete without some of the trimmings that contribute attractiveness and enjoyment. But just as it would be foolish to make a house out of wallpaper when there is no foundation and no walls, so it is foolish to concentrate only on the trimmings of religion while neglecting the essentials.

If we are not content with the way our lives are going and wish to consider turning them over to the care of God, we must be careful that we do not limit ourselves to our own understanding of God.

In many areas of life, we read instruction manuals and get instruction from experts. If you know nothing about the way an automobile engine is put together and operates and yet you try to make your car run more smoothly by tampering with the engine, you will certainly end up with a greater problem than you had.

If one is willing to get direction from an expert when it comes to a car engine, why should one be hesitant to accept guidance from an expert in the operation of one's life?

One of the most difficult challenges facing the human being is accepting the superiority of divine wisdom. So many things happen that are so unnecessary and even downright unfair that it makes one wonder why a supreme, intelligent being would allow these things to occur. Given that humans have free will to do right or wrong, it is not too difficult to understand that tragedies can happen as a result of human action, but when we see suffering and tragedy resulting from floods, earthquakes, famine, and other natural causes, we may ask "Why? Why does God allow these things to happen?"

We are not alone in asking this question. The greatest theologians and philosophers have grappled with the question of why bad things happen to good people, and no one has yet provided a fully satisfactory answer. Some have been so upset by this problem that they have denied the existence of God. However, it has been wisely said that if God exists, human suffering does not make any sense; if God does not exist, *nothing* makes any sense.

Scientific and philosophic enlightenment in the mid-twentieth century gave rise to the "God is dead" idea. Man had achieved

such mastery over the elements that he saw no need for any supreme being.

Man's omnipotence is often short-lived. Circumstances may bring a man to recognize that all of his scientific genius and achievements notwithstanding, he is still relatively impotent. There are no atheists in foxholes.

People reject God as long as they feel they are in full control of their lives. If we succeed in adopting steps one and two, step three is a natural consequence.

Turning one's life over to the care of God may be difficult, even for people who believe in a supreme being. So many things that are very important to us must be completely insignificant to an infinitely great supreme being. The universe is billions of light years in expanse. There are billions of stars that dwarf our sun. On a celestial sphere, the earth is so tiny that it would not be represented by even a microscopic dot. Is it logical, then, for one to turn one's life over to a Power who concerns Himself with supergalaxies?

The answer is that, relative to infinity, small and large are equally significant or insignificant. Infinity divided by .00001 or by 1,000,000 gives the same result.

Whatever occupies the interest of the supreme being is of no greater consequence if it is immensely large or infinitesimally small. Once we posit the infinity of God and that there are things in which God does take interest, it is perfectly logical that He is as concerned about the minutest of human problems as by the greatest of cosmic events. It is therefore also perfectly reasonable to turn one's life over to His care.

Many people have difficulty with step three. Even though they have recognized that the way they have been running their lives has been disastrous and that the only way out is to turn will and life over to the care of God, they are nevertheless worried or frightened. What happens if what God wants does not coincide with what *they* want?

Of course, such thinking indicates that one has not really accepted the difficult conclusion that one's own will has wreaked havoc with one's life and is essentially still saying "I want what I want, and I would like a god who would comply with my desires." It is therefore time to go back to steps one and two and face the fact that one's own desires have been very ill advised. Only when convinced of this can one go on to step three.

Prayers may seem quite innocent until one realizes that they may be answered.

Too often we only give lip service to our values. We should pray for divine guidance and have sufficient belief in the ideals we espouse to wish to actualize them, even though this might deprive us of things we have been considering desirable.

*T*he God to whose care we turn our lives over must be a God who cares about us, feels for us, watches over us, and wishes to guide us to ultimate happiness. This is a very personal God.

As we develop institutions of religion, whether churches or synagogues or religious schools, we run into the problem of supporting such places. Buildings cost money to erect and operate, and people must be paid for their services.

A need for money to operate religious facilities may make religion appear commercial.

There are many fine and dedicated religious institutions that maintain a sincere care for their adherents. Unfortunately, there are also people who will exploit religion for their own needs.

We should not let the existence of unscrupulous people make us skeptical about religion as a whole. A bit of searching should help us find the real thing.

One of the most heartwarming of experiences is observing by people in the twelve-step program the tolerance of other people's high-

er power. Catholic and Jew, Protestant and Muslim, Atheist and Buddhist—all must learn to tolerate the beliefs of others.

When we look at the history of the world, it is painful to note how much human suffering is the result of people's unwillingness to tolerate other people's religions.

"Believe the way I do or you will be expelled or killed." How foolish!

Among small children we can hear "My father can lick your father!" Wouldn't it be wonderful if, as adults, we really grew up and let others be happy with their Father?

Violet, like Lucy, defends her fragile self-esteem with an attitude of superiority. She extends this defense to include her father, who must be greater than other fathers.

Charlie Brown is not threatened by this. He has a good father. He knows his father loves him and provides for him, and that is all that counts. So what if someone can find some imperfection in his father?

If Charlie Brown had challenged Violet, a holy war would have erupted. Charlie Brown's response totally disarms Violet, who must concede that they both have good fathers.

We can have God as we understand Him and others can have God as they understand Him.

The alcoholic who looks at his personal life during a sober moment may recognize the ruin that his drinking has caused and the shambles it has made of his life, but this is not always so evident when alcohol is not the culprit. Yet if we listen to the recovering alcoholic, who is likely to describe his behavior while drinking as "self-will run riot," we can borrow the phrase and see whether some of the problems we are encountering in our own lives might also be due to "self-will run riot," even if it does not involve drinking.

Sometimes it is difficult to see this in ourselves, but it is not too difficult if we look around us: a nation with abundant blessings, yet with many people living in poverty, many people ruining their lives with drugs and alcohol, and crime so rampant that we cannot keep up with building prisons to house the criminals. Beyond our borders there is strife and bloodshed virtually everywhere. What is this all due to if not "self-will run riot"?

What would the world be like if we were to set our own wills aside? The history of mankind makes this goal a fantasy, a wishful thinking.

But if the will of the whole world or a whole nation cannot be reined in, what about a smaller unit, like the family, or perhaps myself?

4

We Made a Searching and Fearless Moral Inventory of Ourselves

Alcoholics who recover via Alcoholics Anonymous are very fortunate, because they are required to take a personal inventory. Most other people can go through life without ever taking a careful personal inventory, because there is nothing that compels them to do so.

To stop drinking is just one part of recovery. The problem is not just alcohol, it is alcoholism. When the drinking stops, the ism remains until it is taken care of.

That ism is comprised of all the inappropriate behavior the person must correct if he or she is to be something more than just abstinent. People who never had a problem with alcohol may nevertheless have the ism, and just as much need to overcome it.

The ism is essentially comprised of the seven cardinal sins or faults human beings may have: pride, greed, lust, anger, gluttony, envy, and sloth. Obviously, these can be just as destructive to the nonalcoholic as to the drinker. By pride we mean false pride, the need to justify oneself and the inability to admit a mistake. These seven traits are interconnected, because it is often false pride that results in anger. A person who has false pride is apt to frequently feel angry because he was not given what he feels is his just due. He is apt to take as a personal insult many things that were never intended as such. Pride may stimulate greed and envy because the person may think he deserves much more than he has. Some of the seven traits take on their destructive character when they are indulged in to excess. For example, normal eating that provides the body with the nutrition it requires is healthy. Overindulgence in food beyond what the body needs is gluttony. Appropriate sexual relations are healthy, but indulging in sex to excess is the vice of lust.

How are we to know whether any facet of our behavior is healthy or excessive? The only way is to take an inventory of ourselves, sitting down with paper and pencil and actually writing down what we have done and how we have done it. This may be a painstaking process and one we might wish to avoid or at least delay, but there is no way around it. If we wish to improve the quality of our lives, an inventory is absolutely essential.

If we look at those aspects of our lives that are causing us problems, we are likely to find them resulting from one or more of these negative character traits.

Recognition of what we did wrong is painful, and the human psyche tries to avoid emotional pain every bit as much as it tries to avoid physical pain. We thus tend to rationalize our behavior and justify the things we have done. We project blame onto others when things go wrong. These two psychological defenses, rationalization and projection, prevent us from owning up to our shortcomings and taking the necessary steps to overcome them. Only by taking a personal inventory can we eliminate those character traits that are destructive to our well-being.

Mistakes are not one-time occurrences. Human beings are fallible, and we are always prone to error. Therefore, taking a personal inventory should not be a one-time event. Periodically, at least one time each year, we should take an accurate personal inventory.

*F*alse pride can get in the way of everything. We all have imperfections. We may even have been born with some traits that affect our behavior. Curbing these traits and converting any negative ones to positives is what growth and maturation is all about.

Yes, you can help it if you were born with crabby genes. You can learn how not to be crabby. You can develop a more pleasant disposition.

But if you don't work to improve your character and you find that people don't like you, you are apt to let your false pride convince you that they are jealous of you.

Taking a fearless inventory and becoming willing to look at ourselves more critically can help us correct undesirable personality features. Failure to do so can result in our being so arrogant that we turn people off.

*R*ejections of any kind are painful. We are hurt if the publisher does not think our manuscript has merit. We are hurt when the person we are courting does not think we are desirable. We are hurt when the employer does not think we have the qualifications for the job.

The constructive approach is to analyze ourselves critically. What is it that I should be doing that I'm not doing?

Lucy likes Schroeder, but Schroeder does not reciprocate.

Schroeder's first love is music. Lucy, however, cannot tell a bust of Beethoven from one of George Washington and refers to a symphony as being written in the key of Asia Minor, yet cannot see why Schroeder does not take a serious interest in her.

Instead of trying to improve her deficiencies in order to gain Schroeder's affection, Lucy harps on what she feels are her assets and is critical of Schroeder for being remiss in not appreciating them.

Taking a personal inventory can help us pinpoint our deficiencies and enable us to correct them.

*I*t is said that a woman once chastised Noah Webster for including obscene words in the dictionary.

"You looked for them, madam," Webster responded calmly.

It is easy to blame others and to disown any responsibility for something. This woman obviously looked up the nasty words, but rather than be critical of herself for thinking of them she found fault with someone else.

Patty's version:

> The television, newspapers, radio, and magazines distracted me.

A fearless moral inventory would read:

> I watched television instead of studying.
> I listened to the radio instead of studying.
> I read the sport pages and magazines instead of studying.

If we take responsibility for our behavior, we can set things straight. If we blame others, then we absolve ourselves from making any changes. The quality of our lives will improve when others stop their pernicious behavior.

Patty will have to wait for good grades until radio, television, newspapers, and the magazine industry all are defunct.

Good luck, Patty.

Some people seem to have no difficulty making a moral inventory. They just make someone else's inventory rather than their own. Inasmuch as step four requires making a *fearless* inventory, it obviously refers to our own inventory. There is certainly no need for courage when making someone else's.

Perhaps it would be wise to conceptualize one's life as a field trip. We are here to observe everything around us and to learn from what we observe so that we might put it to use.

Instead of making important observations one could use to improve oneself, some people waste their time observing everybody else and suggesting what others should do to become better.

While field trips can be enjoyable, their prime function is educational. While life can be enjoyable, its prime function is *self-*improvement.

The expression *fearless inventory* suggests that one must brace oneself with courage for the ordeal. The apprehension may come from two sources, which are strangely enough contradictory but may coexist in one person.

There may be fear that one will discover positive qualities in one-

self about which one was unaware. Why may this be frightening? Because having the capability to perform carries with it the responsibility to perform. One cannot then cop out and say "I am unable to do that."

There can also be fear that one will discover that one does not have the "smarts" to do well. This feeling of inadequacy is usually unfounded and has its origin in a distorted self-perception.

As objective observers, we know Charlie to be lovable. If Charlie often fails, it is because he does not believe in himself. Of course, having Lucy as his psychiatrist doesn't help much, because Lucy bolsters her own sagging self-esteem by deflating everyone around her.

Don't be afraid of making an inventory. Don't stand in the express line, because you have much more than six items, and if anyone tries to tell you otherwise, it is because they are trying to inflate their ego at your expense.

If we wish to make constructive changes in our lives, the place to begin is with an inventory. It is foolish to go shopping for groceries without knowing what you already have and what you need. Otherwise, you might return with six more cans of tomato soup to add to the twenty cans that are already in your cabinet and without the milk for the empty refrigerator.

Taking a grocery inventory is a minor chore, but taking a personality inventory can be quite difficult. We are likely to discover things we would like to forget are there as well as empty spaces where important items are missing. When a task is formidable, we have to muster the strength and courage to complete it. Otherwise we will walk away from it at the first sign of discomfort.

Incidentally, we too often make unwarranted presumptions. Isn't

it just possible that Linus might have some nice things to say about Lucy, both as a person *and* as a sister? Why does Lucy jump to the conclusion that what he would say about her is negative?

If you take inventory of all that has accumulated in your attic for the past twenty years, you will indeed find some worthless junk that should be discarded, but you are also likely to find many nice things you forgot were there—and perhaps even some valuable antiques.

We all have accumulated stuff in our lifetimes. We may have many pleasant memories, nice things we would be proud of and could enjoy if we searched for them and dusted them off. The problem is that they are tucked away among piles of things we would rather forget. So we fail to retrieve the good stuff because we want to avoid the bad.

That's why making an inventory must be done fearlessly. But if we really want to make changes, an inventory is a prerequisite.

Sometimes people who try to make a personal inventory come up with very little of substance. They can't understand why they are not making any greater headway in their personality development.

One night a man observed a young boy on all fours looking for something at the street corner.

"Did you lose something?" he asked.

"Yes," the boy answered. "I lost a half-dollar down there," pointing to a place half a block away.

"Then why are you looking for it here?"

"Because the light is better!"

It is only human nature to wish to avoid discomfort. If looking in one place becomes unpleasant, we reflexively shy away from that place and begin to look elsewhere.

Unfortunately, we may expend a great deal of time and effort in

futility. Even much faith and patience are wasted if you dig for Egyptian coins in the wrong desert.

If you are aware that you might have a tendency to look for something where the light is better rather than where you lost it because you like to do what is easier, you may come to the correct conclusion that perhaps you had better check with someone who knows better and who can direct you to look in the right place.

*M*any—probably most—emotional disorders are the result of people having unwarranted negative feelings about themselves. I address this theme in my book *Like Yourself and Others Will, Too* (Prentice-Hall, 1978).

A person who is down on himself (however mistaken his impression may be, to him they represent reality) behaves according to what he perceives reality to be. What use is there in trying to make friends if you think no one will like you? What use is there in asking for a date if you feel you are certain to be refused?

Charlie doesn't believe there is a chance that the little red-haired girl will like him. He avoided making contact with her, then realizes that he avoided her because of how he feels about himself. Now he has one more reason for not liking himself—his inability to assert himself. This is an excellent example of how the negative self- image reinforces itself in a vicious cycle.

Making an inventory is the first step in a more accurate self-awareness. The results of the fourth step have to be submitted to an outside observer for some objective feedback (fifth step). This may help us see how mistaken we were about ourselves: that we were unjustly harsh on ourselves in our self-evaluation.

5

We Admitted to God, to Ourselves, and to Another Human Being the Exact Nature of Our Wrongs

In step four we try to make an honest appraisal of ourselves. In step five we share that appraisal by admitting to God and to another person the wrongs we have done. Admitting to God doesn't require much discussion. Inasmuch as it is done very privately, it does not present too much of a problem. What is much more difficult is sharing some of our innermost secrets with another human being.

Many of the emotional problems that exist in the alcoholic can also be found in many nonalcoholics. One physician who is now more than twenty-five years sober says: "I did not take my first drink until I was seventeen, and I did not start my heavy drinking until I was twenty-seven. But I remember that when I was nine years old, I felt different. I thought I was different than the other kids. When I would walk into a room full of people, I felt I did not belong."

This feeling of isolation, of not belonging, occurred many years before the drinking began and was not a consequence of the alcoholism. This same feeling of isolation is also present in people who never drank and is a source of much difficulty in interpersonal relations.

Human beings are gregarious animals. With rare exceptions, humans crave the companionship of other humans. When a person isolates himself and withdraws from interaction with other people, it is not because he does not want their company but because he feels he does not belong with them. He feels that people will not want his company and will reject him and, to avoid the pain of rejection, avoids contact with other people.

A great sense of relief comes when a person realizes that he is not as different as he thought—that other people have the same drives, fears, lusts, hates, and other emotions that have made him so self-conscious. When we hear ourselves relate the ideas and feelings we have been harboring as the terrible secrets of our lives, two things happen. First, by simply talking about them, we defuse them and eliminate the magnification that has resulted from their fermenting for years in the deep recesses of our minds. Second, we discover that we share these ideas and feelings with others. We are not alone; and, just as others have been able to grow through these ideas and feelings, so can we.

There is another advantage of sharing our self-appraisal with another person. Emotionally charged ideas and feelings are subject to considerable distortion. We cannot possibly be objective when our emotions are involved. We therefore need some objective observer who is not affected by our emotional distortions to provide a different perspective and help us see things in a different light.

Step five is extremely important. If it is done often enough, it can also be very economical. It may save the cost of paying an expensive psychotherapist to listen.

Following the twelve steps helps us improve our personality. Even if we recognize that some of our behavior is improper and stop doing wrong things, we may be left with an uncomfortable personality. For example, if the alcoholic stops drinking and does nothing more to change his personality, he may become very with-

drawn, because he was dependent on the alcohol for his socialization.

So use the steps not only to alter your outward behavior but also to feel more secure and positive about yourself.

Why is step five necessary after making an inventory in step four? Because there are times when our character defects are so obvious that we cannot fail to see them. However, we are apt to interpret them as virtues rather than as faults.

There are people who pride themselves on how cleverly they can lie or how they have been able to pull off crooked deals without being detected. Their success at what they are doing blinds them to the true nature of their behavior.

This is why we run our self-appraisal before the eyes of an objective observer, who can help point out our self-deceptions.

Pig-pen cannot deny that he is filthy, but since he has this strange penchant for wallowing in mud, he sees being dirty as handsome rather than as loathsome.

Obviously, showing Pig-pen what he looks like in the mirror accomplishes nothing. He already knows that he is dirty. He just thinks that dirty is beautiful.

Perhaps, if someone we trust and respect provides us a different view of things, we may be able to recognize the truth about ourselves.

We probably all underestimate how powerful our psychological defenses are. If realizing something would give rise to discomfort, our psychological system can conjure up ingenious rationalizations to prevent us from making such a realization.

Avoiding awareness of something is called *denial*. Although it is a classic finding in alcoholism, it is also very commonly found in many other conditions.

Patty's problem is her lack of studying. Instead of applying herself to her schoolwork, Patty watches too much television, then oversleeps and is not only derelict in her homework but also sleeps in class much of the time.

Although this has happened many times and Patty knows it is wrong, she still repeats the behavior and does not learn from her mistakes. She ascribes this to "loss of hindsight." What it is really due to, of course, is that she really does not want to correct the mistake. Patty still wants to stay up late and watch television.

If Marcie were listening to Patty's fifth step, she would say: "No, Patty, you are not losing your hindsight, you just don't want to give up watching television. You have a choice to make. You can choose

television or good grades in school. You cannot have both. Which do you prefer?"

Sometimes, when the facts are placed squarely before us, we make the correct choice.

*I*solation can be very painful, yet we may choose it over interaction with people for fear that others will reject us.

How this fear develops is not always evident. People who grew up in apparently normal homes and were not victims of either material or emotional deprivation may nevertheless develop negative feelings about themselves and believe themselves unlikable.

Having such feelings is bad enough, but not doing anything about them is worse.

Charlie Brown realizes (1) I am lonely and (2) I am intensifying

my loneliness by standing out in the rain alone. What is now need-ed is some action to overcome this loneliness. The fifth step can be a beginning in overcoming this loneliness. By sharing with another person we can learn more about ourselves and also discover that our fears of rejection are unfounded.

If you are running a business, you undoubtedly have some kind of bookkeeping system. In transacting business you have earnings and expenditures; without a system to keep track of them, you would have no way of knowing whether you are making or losing money. Furthermore, you would have no way of knowing which business aspects are profitable and should be developed and expanded, and which aspects are incurring losses and should be discontinued.

How strange that we devote so much attention to our businesses and so little to our personal lives. In the latter, too, there are both "profits" and "losses."

The goal of a person's life should be to refine his or her character and become a better person. Some of the things we do contribute toward that goal, others detract from it. Without an accounting system, how are we to know whether or not we are heading in the right direction and what things are contributing toward or detracting from our ultimate goal?

There is a saying that experience is a hard teacher but that fools will learn no other way. This is a gross fallacy. The wise learn from experience. Fools are those who *do not* learn from experience. There are indeed some things that come to us easily, but for the most part the important things are learned the hard way. When we are infants, our parents tell us not to touch the hot stove, but that does not have much impact. It is only when we do touch the hot stove and discover that it hurts that we learn to avoid contact. This way of learning never ceases throughout life.

We are all far from perfect, and we all make mistakes. We can grow in character if we do not ignore our mistakes but rather admit them and learn from them.

The human mind is a fascinating mechanism. Just as the body has many defense systems that function automatically to ward off disease and anything else that may be noxious to our well-being, so the mind has many defense techniques to protect us from psychological and emotional pain. The problem is that these defensive tactics may actually work against us, as when they prevent us from recognizing our mistakes. When this happens, we are apt to repeat the same mistake until its consequences are so severe we can no longer deny it. That is a very high price to pay for learning, and it would be so much better if there was an easier way.

If we are aware of our tendency to be blind to our own faults, we can appoint someone else to be an outside observer and call our attention to our defects. Such a person would be a true friend.

People who tell us the kinds of things we like to hear about ourselves may be pleasant company, but they contribute little to our character growth. Those people who provide sincere, constructive criticism are our true friends.

Of course, we must be able to accept constructive criticism. If we

react to those people who provide it, they will hold their peace and we will be left with those who provide us with worthless flattery.

Let us assume for the moment that some of your critics are actually malicious. They do not have your best interests at heart. They are simply out to hurt you. They try to focus on your weaknesses and your faults, either to malign, embarrass, or irritate you. . . .

Well, *you* don't have to admire their integrity as Charlie does. You may be justifiably angry. But wait! These bad people are precisely the ones who will detect even your minutest defects and are much more likely to do so than your friends are. So, angry as you may be, listen! "When my enemies arose to condemn me, my ears listened" (Psalms 92:12).

Don't admire their integrity. Just listen.

Let's assume that you wish to point out to a friend of yours something that you feel he should correct. You really want to provide some constructive criticism. Initially, he may be irritated by your efforts to help him. However, if your intentions are sincere, he will overcome his initial reaction and be grateful to you. Be sensitive when you point out someone else's faults.

6

We Were Entirely Ready to Have God Remove All These Defects of Character

Anyone familiar with alcoholics has to stand in total bewilderment, if not awe, before the phenomenon of sobriety. Here you have people who have been unable to stop their clearly destructive drinking for twenty or thirty years. Nothing was able to stop them—neither job loss, nor their loved ones leaving them, nor being in jail, nor having convulsions, nor suffering nearly fatal hemorrhages—nothing. They were driven to drink as if possessed by a demon.

Then something happened—no one knows just what—and now they are not only stone sober, they tell you they no longer have any urge to drink. The very desire for alcohol is gone. The insane craving that dominated them for decades no longer exists. How did that happen? If you push them hard enough for an explanation, they are likely to say: "One day I reached a point of such desperation that I cried out to God—to a God that I never believed in—'If you are up there, help me! Take this curse off me.' And He did."

If you have seen as many alcoholics as I have, you are hard-pressed to come to any other conclusion. Only some divine act can explain these miraculous occurrences.

How does this happen? It happens when one becomes entirely ready to have God remove his defects. *Entirely ready*—these are the key words.

If this works for alcohol, can it work for other problems as well? Is it possible to have other problems lifted from us? I believe it is, but we must be entirely ready. No strings attached. Does this mean that there is a way to achieve perfection? Frankly, yes, but there is no need to worry about that. None of us ever gets entirely ready to be perfect. We will always retain enough imperfections to be normal. Most of us would reject sainthood if it were offered to us on a silver platter.

But while we keep enough imperfections to be normally human, we can use this step to rid ourselves of some things we feel very

deeply about. People have been known to give up destructive habits and behaviors of long standing and not even be subject to their old temptations anymore. All you have to do is reach a point where you are entirely ready—not ninety-nine point nine percent, but one hundred percent—to rid yourself of an objectionable trait.

Just don't fool yourself. You may think you are entirely ready, but you may not really be there yet.

Sometimes we want something so desperately that we want it more than anything else in the world. . . well, almost anything else.

Our behavior attests the degree of our sincerity. If we really want something more than anything else in the world, then we set our priorities in that direction. We must become *entirely ready*.

While we might say we are entirely ready to have all our character defects lifted, this may not be quite true. Most of us would agree that the feeling of being superior to other people is not a commendable one, and that a person should not enjoy dominating others. Yet who can truthfully say they do not enjoy a feeling of superiority, and who can say that they do not enjoy the power of a position of authority?

While we may not be entirely ready to give up all our character defects and while perfection may not be desirable, let alone attainable, there is nothing wrong with setting ideal goals for ourselves. Even people who know they will never become multimillionaires nevertheless try to amass whatever wealth they can. So why not set ideal goals for ourselves?

The recognition that we may not reach the ideal should not stop us from getting as close as possible, nor should we become depressed and frustrated just because we fall short of the ideal mark.

*E*very New Year's Day we hear about New Year's resolutions, and it has become an accepted social ritual that on January first one makes resolutions that have a life expectancy of no longer than one week at the maximum.

"That's it for smoking! As of January first I'm quitting."

"No more hanging around with the guys at the bar after work. I'll be home for supper every day before six."

"I'm through with betting on football games."

"Absolutely no more between-meal snacks for me after New Year's Day. This year the weight goes off and stays off."

Many people really would like to keep their New Year's resolutions. How come virtually no one does so?

Notice that step six is step *six*. In other words, it comes *after* the first five steps.

Changes in habits do not come about easily. Habit and routine have their own inertia, and propel us forward to continue to do whatever we have been doing.

Change requires groundwork. It requires an awareness that we have lost control and have become creatures of habit, that these habits now dominate us. Change requires accepting help from sources outside ourselves. And finally, changes in habits usually require changes in other aspects of our personality.

If you live in New York, say, and make a firm decision to go to Los Angeles, you will nevertheless remain right where you are unless you take the necessary steps of getting the money for a ticket, making the effort of buying the ticket, and actually getting to the airport and getting on the plane. Just deciding to go without taking the necessary steps to get there leaves you right where you were.

*R*emoval of defects of character is not easy. It means making changes in our lifestyle, changes in the way we do things. Making changes requires a great deal of effort, often persistent effort. There is always a tendency to fall back to old habits.

In order to avoid the discomfort of making changes, a person may resign himself to incurability: "I'm too far gone to change. My character is cast in stone."

I remember one young alcoholic woman who persistently requested various tests to see if she had sustained brain damage from her drinking. A bit of investigation revealed that she actually hoped that she would be found to have brain damage, because then she could say "Let me alone. I am hopeless. I have brain damage. You cannot expect me to recover."

There is as much reason to give up at age five as there is at fifty-five—or, to put it another way, it is possible to make changes in character at fifty-five just as one can make changes at age five. It just may take a little more effort.

It is never too late to change.

7

We Humbly Asked Him to Remove Our Shortcomings

*T*he seventh step is related to the first two steps. Following our becoming aware of our powerlessness and the need for some power greater than our own to extricate us from our difficulties, we now humble ourselves and ask for help.

Many people resist asking for help, seeing this as demeaning. Sometimes we hang on to an unrealistic idea of self-sufficiency, refusing to humble ourselves to ask for help. So much unnecessary suffering results from this foolish and obstinate insistence on self-sufficiency! Of course we need help. At one time or another every person needs help, and there is nothing wrong with needing help.

Humility is a wonderful trait. Not only does God love the humble, but other people do, too. The arrogant, who know it all, are obnoxious.

Humility does not mean that one must think of oneself negatively. Not at all. A person should recognize his or her assets and character strengths. Knowing the true facts about oneself is not vanity, but one should realize that one's skills and talents are God-given gifts that should be put to use to the betterment of mankind. One may have true pride in having such gifts, but such true pride leads to humility when one realizes the responsibility and obligations that these gifts impose upon one and that one has probably fallen short of fulfilling them.

Vanity carries with it an attitude of superiority whereby we expect the homage and admiration of others. Humility carries with it an attitude of gratitude for having been endowed with talents and skills and a recognition of the obligation to be of service to others. One can be a great person and be aware of one's greatness, yet be humble.

The truly humble person does not have to avoid asking for help, because it is not demeaning. He can receive help as well as give it.

The vain person is always dissatisfied with what he has. His attitude of superiority makes him feel he deserves more than what he has. He is totally crushed by adversity, because any suffering elicits rage. How dare anyone do this to me? How dare God do this to me? He is so consumed with anger that he becomes hostile and intolerable, let alone miserable with physical symptoms such as the migraine headaches, high blood pressure, and peptic ulcers that are so often the result of internal rage.

The humble person does not think of himself as being unjustly deprived. He can enjoy what he has because he is not ridden with envy of others who may have more. When adversity occurs, he can use his energies to cope instead of being defiantly angry with everyone.

Humility is not just a moral virtue. It is life-saving.

*H*umbly.

Without humility there can be no change, no progress. Why would we wish to change if we are certain that since we can do no wrong, everything we are doing must be right?

When a paranoid psychotic insists that he is being followed, that his house has been bugged, and that the FBI and CIA are watching his every move, there is no budging him with logical arguments or even proof to the contrary. Delusions are fixed ideas not subject to change.

The grandiose delusion that one is perfect and can do no wrong makes change impossible as long as one clings to that delusion.

Lucy's arrogance does not endear her to anyone. She pushes herself on Schroeder, who cannot stand her; she berates Charlie Brown and dominates Linus. Even Snoopy cannot tolerate her.

Lucy alienates everyone, gets depressed, and sulks—but does not change. Why should she change when she is perfect?

Humility allows us to look at ourselves critically and to eliminate those character traits that inhibit our success and serve as barriers between us and other people. Humility promotes enjoyable and healthy relationships.

*I*t is not uncommon to see small children try to assert self-sufficiency and try to do everything themselves. After all, they are little people who live in the world of adults, a world that is furnished according to the needs of adults. When a child has to stand on tiptoe to stretch for the doorknob and even then cannot reach it, he realizes how little he is. No wonder we hear a child squeal with joy when he stands on a chair: "Look how big I am!"

But people who are in fact big should not have to do that. If you feel you are really big, why do you have to point it out to everyone? Why not just assume that everyone will see the true facts?

People who realistically feel good about themselves do not need to assert an attitude of superiority, and when circumstances in life make it necessary for them to ask for help, they have no difficulty in doing so.

Poor Linus. He has not yet learned to tie his shoes and must ask for help.

There is nothing wrong with asking for help, but it does make one feel rather silly if one has been boasting about how one is self-sufficient.

The combination of vanity and reality often results in misery. Humility and reality are pleasantly compatible.

*S*tep seven can come only after step six. We cannot rid ourselves of character defects unless we first recognize that they are indeed defects. The judgment of traits is highly relative: "I am firm in my

convictions. *You* are obstinate. *He* is a stubborn mule." Or: "I am accommodating. *You* are someone who just does not know how to say no. *He* is a spineless jellyfish."

Our lives may be negatively affected by behavior patterns that we do not change because we do not recognize any need for change.

One of the advantages of group therapy or self-help groups is that we expose ourselves to the observations and comments of others. If we are open-minded and do not become defensive, we can gain a great deal by listening to how others observe us. Perhaps what we have considered commendable character traits are defects after all, and we would be so much better off if we rid ourselves of them.

Why is it that, although we sometimes pray for help in overcoming our shortcomings, our prayers seem to go unanswered? After all, if we do make the effort to improve ourselves, don't we deserve the help?

The answer is that our prayers often lack the requisite sincerity. We are at best ambivalent about giving up our shortcomings. Too

often we have been getting some gratification from them and do not wish to give it up.

Even if we do let go completely, we may quickly regret it and try to recapture our shortcomings.

There is only one successful approach. Decide that you wish to rid yourself of your shortcomings and stick by your decision. It is then that prayer is effective.

8

We Made a List of All Persons We Had Harmed, and Became Willing to Make Amends to Them All

Step eight is formidable. No one likes to remember having wronged another person, and it certainly takes a great deal of fortitude to ask another person's forgiveness. In fact, step eight does not even require that we make amends, but only that we become *willing* to make amends. It is recognized that the actual making amends may be so difficult that we may have to have a preparatory phase before actually executing it.

Our psychological systems, like our physiological systems, are programmed to take on a defensive posture in order to avoid pain. When a thought or idea is painful, our psychological systems put in gear the mechanisms that will deny the very existence of the painful thought or strip it of its painful character by justifying it.

Thus, if I harmed someone I might not remember the incident at all or, if I do, I might justify it by saying "He had it coming because of what he did to me." Such defensive thinking is destructive, first, because all untruth is ultimately destructive and, second, because it precludes any possibility of restoring a friendly relationship. If I can admit I did wrong, I can apologize, and there is the possibility of establishing or renewing a friendship. If I maintain an attitude of belligerence, the severance of the relationship cannot be remedied.

Admitting one was wrong is accepting human fallibility. Refusal to admit one did wrong brings us back to the pathologic sense of omnipotence.

Becoming willing to make amends is an acceptance of responsibility, and this is ultimately what separates the men from the boys. Furthermore, becoming willing to make amends means that we are willing to ask for forgiveness for our misdeeds, and if we can grasp the concept of forgiveness, we also become ready to forgive others for what they might have done to us.

Finally, it we make an honest list of all persons we have harmed, we are likely to discover that we may have harmed people by dereliction in meeting our obligations or by failure to come to their assistance when we had the capacity to do so. As we become aware of our derelictions, we can take steps to permit such occurrences in the future, and this enhances our personality growth and happiness as well as enables us to do things for others.

This is as good a place as any to expand on rationalization.

When you want to do something badly enough, any excuse will do. Strangely, an excuse that appears patently absurd to everyone else will appear perfectly sensible to the person who needs it.

For example, if you ask an alcoholic what made him start drinking after he had stopped for a while, he will give you reasons that may be hilarious but that he sincerely believes were adequate reasons to drive him to drink.

Linus wants to suck his thumb and watch TV instead of being outdoors. His rationalization is one that any alcoholic would be proud of.

It is never good to be deceptive, but if you succeed at cleverly deceiving yourself, what have you gained? You have become the victim of your own cunning.

Sometimes we are overcome by temptation and do something we should not have done. That is understandably human. If we recognize we did something wrong, we can take proper precautions to avoid a recurrence. However, if we deceive ourselves into thinking that what we did was right, we will never correct ourselves.

Rationalization and Projection

If you have ever been involved in an automobile accident, you know what rationalization and projection are. The driver who made a turn without signaling or pulled away from the curb without checking for oncoming traffic accuses the other guy of driving too fast and being the cause of the accident.

So many times we become defensive when we are obviously at

fault. Instead of admitting a mistake we try to blame things on others.

Lucy was grossly negligent, not paying the slightest attention to what was going on in the ball game. Yet when reprimanded, she completely ignores her dereliction and instead finds fault with Charlie Brown for shouting at her.

To err is human. It is even human to make stupid mistakes. But unless we own up to them, we don't stand a chance of improving ourselves.

When we think of people we may have harmed, we generally think of acts of commission, something we did that offended or injured them. We may not realize that acts of omission can be just as serious. Failure to appreciate or acknowledge a favor, failure to come to someone's aid when it was within our means to do so, or failure to speak up in someone's defense are examples of such acts of omission.

Passive harm can be every bit as painful and injurious as active harm. Since passive injuries are less likely to be remembered, we would do well to make a daily list of our actions and inactions so we can become aware of our passive derelictions.

Lucy has not uttered one word, not one single word, yet Linus walks away crushed. All that was necessary was a simple statement like "Don't be silly. I'm just trying to see how bugs behave," and Linus would have been spared a deflating insult.

While silence is indeed golden, there are times when it can be devastating.

We need to make amends for things we did not do as well as for those we did.

One of the features that distinguishes adulthood from childhood is the acceptance of responsibility. An immature individual cannot be held fully responsible, and a grown-up who refuses to accept responsibility is psychologically immature.

Humans are subject to error, and the realization that one made a mistake should not be a devastating experience.

Some people seem unable to own up to having made a mistake.

They defend their mistakes and rationalize their actions to convince themselves as well as others that they are blameless.

In *When Do the Good Things Start?*, Lucy is shown to be a person who is very insecure and has low self-esteem but covers up this feeling with an attitude of superiority and infallibility.

The need to feel that one is beyond blame and to escape responsibility is indicative of low self-esteem. People who truly think well of themselves are able to accept that they may have been at fault.

Willingness to recognize one's mistakes and make amends for them is a sign of maturity.

9

We Made Direct Amends to Such People Wherever Possible, Except When to Do So Would Injure Them or Others

One of the areas that has been subject to confusion among both the laity and the psychological profession is guilt. There is no question that lingering guilt is a destructive feeling and can take a heavy emotional toll on a person. However, the methods of ridding oneself of guilt require careful examination.

Guilt can be either healthy or unhealthy. Healthy guilt results when we do something we should not have done, something that is indeed wrong, something in violation of the principles of decency

and morality. This kind of guilt is healthy, just as pain is a healthy sensation when it signals that our body is in danger of harm from either an internal or external source. We often refrain from doing something improper because we do not wish to suffer the guilt a particular act would produce.

If we have indeed done something wrong, the resultant guilt stimulates us to take corrective action. We resolve not to repeat the particular act, and we can take appropriate action to try to right whatever wrongs we have committed. Such corrective action relieves the feeling of guilt.

There is also a pathological, unhealthy kind of guilt, which a person may feel even though he has not done anything wrong. This second type of guilt requires professional help to determine how it came about and how to divest oneself of it. Unhealthy guilt is characteristically not relieved by apologies or acts of atonement and expiation. You cannot atone for a nonexistent transgression.

How do unhealthy guilt feelings come about? The causes are many and varied. Our minds may play tricks on us, and if something harmful happens to a person at whom we were angry, we may think our hostile wish brought on the misfortune. This is referred to in psychology as "magical thinking" and is a residue of a very juvenile type of thinking that is normal in children but should disappear as we mature. If this magical thinking persists, we are apt to have unwarranted guilt feelings.

At any rate, if we find ourselves tormented by guilt feelings, we would be wise to get some expert opinions. If the guilt is real, then following step nine is the correct approach.

One of the reasons a person may have unwarranted guilt feelings is so low an opinion of himself that he thinks he always does things

wrong. Some children, made to feel responsible for everything that goes wrong, can never shake that feeling as they grow up.

Sometimes a person has made so many mistakes that he assumes he always does things wrong, even when he has done something right.

Lucy regularly misses the ball, and Charlie regularly reprimands her for doing so. Lucy always seems to find an excuse for missing the ball, but the very fact that she has to rationalize indicates that she feels badly about it.

Lucy's habitual errors lead her to feel that she has committed another error even though the game hasn't started yet.

Take a look at the kinds of things about which you feel guilty. There may well be some guilt you are carrying unnecessarily.

Sometimes we do things that offend another person. Even if we do so inadvertently, we should at least have the consideration to tell the victim that we are sorry for any distress we may have caused him or her. If circumstances are such that we can redress any wrong we have done, we certainly have the responsibility to do so.

It is nice of Charlie to apologize, but he also could have brought Snoopy a bowl of water.

Sometimes it is relatively easy to amend something we have done, and at other times it may be more difficult, but we should always try.

If making amends is somehow injurious, we should avoid adding injury through our benevolent intentions.

How can making amends be injurious to anyone? This question raises some very thorny ethical problems. For example, a woman who is happily married and has two children is tormented by the fact that she never revealed to her husband that she had a child out of wedlock and had given it up for adoption. She feels that she has been dishonest with her husband by not completely revealing her past, and she feels compelled to make amends to him by telling all. However, knowing his attitude, she has little doubt that he will be furious and will undoubtedly divorce her. She is willing to accept what she feels is coming to her, but is deeply concerned that the children will suffer needlessly. Does she have the right to disrupt

the children's lives? People may take different sides, but the point here is that sometimes making amends can be injurious.

Apologizing to a person may seem innocent enough, but even then one must be careful how one does so. Sometimes one can apologize in a manner that aggravates the problem.

Lucy feels bad about her sometimes uncontrollable screaming. Her method of apology, however, ends up being just as abrasive as her critical comments.

Sometimes it is better to stay silent.

Making amends should be a result of the realization that a wrong needs to be righted, that an injury should be redressed. If one apologizes to or otherwise compensates someone for harm done to him

because of an ulterior motive, that is not really making amends—it is simply furthering one's own selfish interests.

Affected amends are often as apparent and flagrantly absurd as they are worthless.

*I*f we harm others financially, it is appropriate to offer to make restitution. If we hurt someone's feelings, a sincere expression of regret is all that is needed. Giving the person an opportunity to take revenge is not only unnecessary and foolish but also encourages the other person to redress a wrong by committing another wrong.

People who think every wrong requires punishment have no concept of forgiveness. They are likely to consider God punitive because they ascribe to Him their own ideas of how to react to commitment of a misdeed.

These people are likely to be chronically unhappy. If something bad happens to them, they immediately conclude that it was God's way of punishing them and then protest that they were punished too harshly and that God is unfair. If nothing bad happens to them, they suffer the anxiety and suspense of expecting disaster to descend upon them at any moment.

We must learn to forgive and to be able to accept the forgiveness of others.

*T*his is something that does not occur too frequently but does happen often enough to warrant our attention.

Suppose I do something nasty to someone. For example, I know that my friend is negotiating to buy a house and I buy it from under his nose. Not exactly a nice thing to do to a friend. A short time later something happens to the house—say, a fire or a flood or something else that is not fully covered by insurance—and I lose my investment. Initially the friend may have been angry at me, but now he is grateful that I saved him from a misfortune. Do I still owe him an apology?

We must remember that we are not God, nor do we have prophetic foresight. We cannot foretell how things will turn out. All we can judge ourselves by is what we do. If we do something offensive

to someone, we owe him or her an apology regardless of the consequences of our act. We cannot escape our obligation to make amends by claiming that what we did was ultimately to the other person's advantage.

Our psychological defenses are very cunning. In defending our actions, we sometimes deceive ourselves as well as others.

Suppose someone confronts you about something uncomplimentary you said about him. If this is true, admit it. Admitting it will help avoid repeating the behavior, and in all likelihood the other person will accept a sincere apology. This honesty provides a feeling of personal dignity as well as the respect and trust of others.

But what if we do not own up to our actions?

We might try to deny our behavior and perhaps tell the person that what he heard was all wrong: "It was other people that said those things about you. I was the one who came to your defense."

Whether we try to cover up our behavior or otherwise shirk the responsibility for our actions, we are left with self-loathing if we have any sense of conscience at all. Furthermore, the truth is likely to come out sooner or later.

Never defend a mistake. It simply does not pay.

10

We Continued to Take Personal Inventory and When We Were Wrong Promptly Admitted It

When we reach a point of crisis in life, we generally make some significant changes. We may have gone through a business failure, an unworkable marriage, or come to the realization that we were drinking too much. In any case, a constructive change requires an analysis of the past and a correction of those factors that led to the crisis.

However, analyzing the past is not enough. The realization of what mistakes were made in the past is no guarantee against their recurrence. Quite the contrary, there is a likelihood that we will repeat the same mistakes or do something very similar. Sigmund Freud gave this tendency the name *repetition compulsion*, as if there were something driving us to repeat the mistakes of the past.

The safeguard against repeating previous mistakes is to maintain a state of alertness. However, since we may be unaware that we are doing the same things again, it will help to have the vigilance of an outside observer who can call to our attention those things that we fail to see ourselves. Of course, we must then be ready to admit the mistakes that are brought to our attention, because otherwise we will go down the same path of failure again. It is important that when we take stock of ourselves we do not focus exclusively on the negative. There are many things we do that are right, and although awareness of these should not cause us to be vain, we should not underestimate ourselves either. Just as to run a successful business you must know what is causing losses so that these can be avoided and what is bringing in profits so that these can be enlarged upon, so it is with our personal lives. We must know what not to do and what to do more of.

Anyone operating a business takes time out periodically to evaluate progress and to discover the pros and cons. We should be no less interested in the successful course of our personal lives and apply the same techniques.

*I*t is no accident that this step is the tenth. It comes quite late in the series because it must be preceded by the considerable growth and personality maturation that is achieved by mastery of the nine earlier steps. Even then it is difficult enough.

How different the world would be if more people lived according to this tenth step and admitted when they were wrong! The tragedy of refusing to recognize one's mistake and admitting them is no less in one's personal life than in political life, where calamity has befallen those who have tried to cover up mistakes.

There appears to be a natural tendency to defend one's actions. This may lead to the most absurd rationalizations, yet a person may be so defensive of his position that he is unable to see the true nature of his actions.

The person who is convinced that he cannot possibly do any wrong is doomed to repeat his mistakes, since there is hardly any possibility of correcting something one feels needs no correction. For a time one can maintain the facade of self-assurance, but this attitude is bound to be ultimately ruinous. Mistakes have a way of compounding themselves and eventually bring about such devastation that even the most self-righteous must own up to their failures. Unfortunately, this is a very costly way of coming to grips with reality.

Living according to step ten can make life so much easier.

*S*ome people may be so defiant and adamant in their refusal to yield that they contradict facts: "My mind is made up. Don't bother me with evidence." Most people are not so brazen as to defy fact, but when it comes to matters of opinion, since there is nothing to coerce them to change their minds they may refuse to listen to logical reasoning. Excellent examples are the Renaissance Church's refusal to accept the Copernican theory and the insistence of some people that the world was flat even after the globe had been circumnavigated.

Individual as well as world progress is facilitated when people agree to examine their opinions and are flexible enough to consider that they might be wrong.

The tenth step is so important in recovery from addictive diseases because in order to maintain one's recourse to alcohol, drugs,

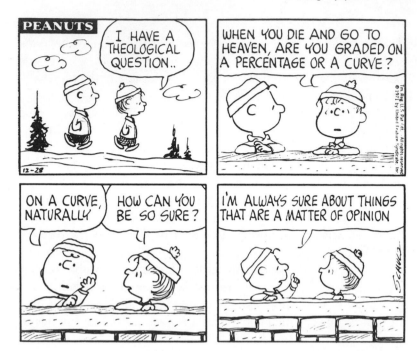

or excessive food the addicted individual erects an impenetrable barrier to opinions other than his own. The recovery that is initiated with steps one through five can be sustained only if one thinks "In my days of active addiction, I used to be absolutely certain that I was so right, even though I now realize how wrong I had been. I am still vulnerable to faulty opinions, and I must be prepared to admit that I may be wrong."

This is a healthy attitude for everyone to assume, whether or not one has had an addiction problem.

I have observed a strange phenomenon. People embark on a course that holds great promise for a favorable change in their lives, and just as they seem to be approaching success they do something to scuttle it and to undermine everything they worked for. It's amazing!

It may be the alcoholic who has the first experience of extended sobriety and discovers his family loves him and that his worth is so much improved. It may be the person who starts a business that proves a profitable venture. It may be the student who applies himself to his courses and reverses his failing grades. Lo and behold, they pull failure out of the very jaws of success.

Discovering that what we are doing now is right and what we had been doing previously was wrong means that we should abandon our ways of the past and adopt a new way.

While logic tells us that this is precisely what we should do, the tug of the habits of the past is extraordinarily strong, so strong that it may override logic and pull us back into the defeating lifestyle of the past.

Like Violet, we may be threatened by the awareness that good sense requires that we change our lifestyle. Much like Violet, we may abort success when it requires such change.

Unless we remain on the alert not to repeat errors of the past, there is a high likelihood that we will do so in spite of our resolve to do otherwise.

To err is human; to repeat the same mistakes over and over again is stupid. Yet, if we observe both ourselves and others, we are sure to note that people do fall into the trap of repeating their mistakes. Someone wisely said "It isn't that it's one thing after another. It's the same damn thing over and over again!"

Can the pitfall of repetitious mistakes be avoided? Of course it can. We simply have to be alert and honest.

The alcoholic is the prototype of a person who, although he gets the same disastrous results every time he drinks, deludes himself that "This time it will be different."

Are we pleased with the way our lives have been going? If the answer is negative, there is only one solution. Change!

Obviously, one must give careful thought as to how and what one should change, but one should not be foolish enough to think that persisting in what one has been doing will somehow give different results than in the past.

Some people have a propensity for looking at themselves in a bad light, focusing only on their liabilities and being oblivious of their assets.

We do many good things each day and we should be aware of them. If indeed we discover that we did something wrong, and as a result of this discovery we can take proper precautions to avoid doing it again, this has been a valuable learning experience and should always be considered a positive experience.

Lucy is hardly helpful in building anyone's self-esteem, but even without her criticism Charlie Brown can hardly get beyond giving

himself credit that he did not do anything wrong. He is unable to find positives about himself.

Discovering that one has done something right serves as a stimulus to do more good things. If we develop Charlie Brown's negative attitude we are likely to think "Oh, what's the use?"

Look for the positives in yourself and you will find them.

If I were to choose a single character defect that causes people more misery than any other, it would be the *inability to admit a mistake.*

We are all human and we all err. If we realize we are fallible, we are able to live with our own mistakes and forgive those of others. Furthermore, recognizing our human fallibility, we will assume that others are much like us and that they too will forgive our mistakes.

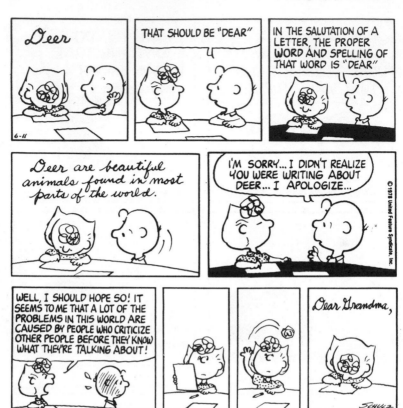

However, if we refuse to admit mistakes, we are unlikely to forgive ourselves—and, what is perhaps worse, others will not forgive us if we do not own up to having been wrong. Recent history has dramatically demonstrated the folly of cover-ups. How much suffering, both individual and national, would have been averted with the simple words "I made a mistake. I was wrong."

Sally makes a mistake and extracts an apology from Charlie Brown. Charlie wasted effort in the cover-up. Charlie Brown walks away feeling embarrassed, and Sally cannot feel good about having hurt Charlie Brown when he was indeed right.

There were probably eleven commandments rather than ten. The first one was "Thou shall not defend a mistake." Moses assumed that this was so obvious that it really did not require being recorded.

Too bad.

11

We Sought Through Prayer and Meditation to Improve Our Conscious Contact With God as We Understood Him, Praying Only for Knowledge of His Will for Us and the Power to Carry That Out

Why is it important to pray for the knowledge of God's will? Why isn't my own will good enough? And if my own will is not good enough, why is God's will the only alternative?

The answer to the second question is rather simple. If my own will were that wholesome, why do I find myself in the difficulties I am in now? Is it really everyone else's fault that I did not get what I wanted and what I justly deserve, or could it be that what I wanted was not really desirable or even realistic?

The third question is somewhat more difficult. Granted that my own will may have been misguided, why can I not adopt some other will? Why does it have to be God's will?

The fact is that if we were able to set our own wills aside, we could live much more meaningful and productive lives. With our personal biases and desires out of the picture we could do more things for the betterment of the community and mankind as a whole, and that would be a major achievement.

Yet there is something lacking even in this. There is a story about two men who were brought before a judge, having been arrested for loitering.

"What were you doing when you were arrested?" the judge asked the first man.

"Nothing," the man answered.

The judge then turned to the second man and asked: "And what were you doing when you were arrested?"

The second man pointed to his friend: "I was helping him."

It seems rather evident that as noble as it is to help another person, if that other person is doing nothing, the helper is not really achieving anything either.

If everyone in the world were engaged in helping everyone else, it would really be a much more peaceful and beautiful world. Yet we would still be faced with the gnawing question "What is it that we are *all* ultimately doing?"

Nothing is so demoralizing and depressing as a feeling of living in futility. There seems to be an innate desire to feel that one is achieving something and that life has meaning. Many people are so occupied just with the business of surviving that they do not have the time to contemplate the meaning of life. However, as technology has shortened our workweek on the one hand and medical sci-

ence has extended the average lifespan on the other, more people have time to think and hence to reflect on the meaning of life.

Whether step eleven does or does not become your credo is not the issue, but that one must have a purpose in life in order to make life meaningful is beyond doubt.

If we pray for the knowledge of God's will and the power to carry it out, we should be ready for a surprise. Our prayer may be answered. When our prayers are appropriate, God does listen and surprise us with His response.

God's plan for us may be different than what we had in mind. We may have wanted a summer home on the lake, an outboard motor, and plenty of time to go fishing. God's plan may include being of service to others, perhaps by our sharing with them the hope, strength, and courage we developed as we struggled with life's challenges and survived various hardships.

Yes, interesting may hurt. Contrary to Lucy's conclusion, however, boring is not better. One does not become a better fielder when one is not challenged.

God's will may well be for our personal growth, and growing pains are not uncommon. However, we should also be assured that God also provides for us the power to carry out His will.

Sometimes what we consider prayer is really nothing more than bargaining. "If You only get me out of this jam, I promise that . . ." We know only too well how short-lived such promises are.

For prayer to be effective it must be sincere, and sincerity is not bargaining. As long as we bargain, we are still considering ourselves in charge and essentially wish to dictate terms. Too often we don't become aware of the futility of bargaining until our lives have become so unmanageable that we surrender to a higher power.

Peppermint Patty is right. This kind of prayer is always with us. In fact, even if all kinds of religious activity in schools were banned this kind of prayer could continue, because bargaining has nothing to do with religion.

The eleventh step is contingent upon completing the first three steps. Only after having surrendered our own will can prayer cease to be bargaining and become a sincere wish to do what is right instead of what pleases us.

Lincoln is alleged to have said "It makes little difference to me whether God is on my side or on the opposition's side. What is important is that I be on God's side."

Another way to look at it is "Do I want to do the will of God or am I expecting Him to do my will?"

Some people get frustrated and lose faith when God does not

give them what they pray for. Apparently they think that prayer is a polite way of dictating to God what it is He should do.

Of course, if we are certain that we have achieved perfection, that God is just thrilled with everything we do, then there is no need to try to establish conscious contact with Him. Obviously, He would never risk losing contact with someone as terrific as we are.

In *When Do the Good Things Start?* I pointed out that Charlie Brown is plagued with self-doubts and low self-esteem. Lucy, who has the same underlying problem, has defended herself against the pain of low self-esteem by convincing herself of her unparalleled superiority.

As pathetic a character as Charlie Brown may be, he can change for the better. He can be helped to see that he is better than he thinks he is. Lucy is very difficult to help, because she is convinced that she is already perfect.

We should always seek to improve our contact with God, because that means we are seeking to improve ourselves.

One of the most difficult of the steps is to pray only for the knowledge of God's will and the power to carry it out. Taking this seriously means setting aside one's personal strivings, for fame, riches, or whatever, and deciding to want only that which God wants. Since it is not always easy to determine just what God wants, one must pray to be enlightened.

Step eleven is a logical conclusion if one has seriously taken step one. Life usually becomes unmanageable as the result of "self-will run riot." If your own will is getting you into trouble, it is only common sense to set it aside.

Some people who profess to be religious never quite make it to step eleven. God's will is okay *only* if it agrees with their own. They pick and choose which parts of religion they like.

Religion can be wonderful and beautiful. Why is it, then, that when we review world history we see some of the meanest atrocities committed in the name of religion? This occurs when people pick and choose what they like in religion and ignore those religious teachings that do not suit them.

If one discovers that his own lifestyle is ruinous and considers changing to a lifestyle that is based on trying to do the will of God, that is a wise step. If one picks and chooses from religion, one is not doing God's will at all but merely doing one's own will again. Obviously, that will not improve things in the least.

Some people think that praying consists of telling God just what it is that you want and, having told Him so, He is supposed to respond to suit you.

If they do not get what they want, they conclude that God is unfair or that He is against them.

This erroneous conclusion, which has turned some people away from God, is due to the misconception of prayer.

Step eleven defines prayer as a way toward a relationship with God. We are supposed to overcome our defects and become more Godlike. Although we know that no human being can achieve perfection, we should aim to get as close as we can.

True prayer is not for what *we* want, but for God to help us to know what it is that *He* wants of us. If we find our personal wishes and desires frustrated, that should not throw us off. Perhaps this was not what God wanted for us.

One recovering alcoholic woman said "When I lost my job and my marriage broke up, I turned against God. 'Why did You do this to me?' Today I understand that this was His way of taking away those things that I did not have the ability to manage by myself."

Give prayer a chance. Real prayer.

12

Having Had a Spiritual Awakening As the Result of These Steps, We Tried to Carry the Message to Others, And to Practice These Principles in All Our Affairs

*T*here are all kinds of things in life that are enjoyable. Some give us only fleeting pleasure (who can recall a tasty dish that provided us with a delightful experience many years ago?). Other things can provide pleasant memories when we recall them even years later. However, being of help to someone can be a permanent and ongoing source of enjoyment. If I helped someone many years ago, particularly in a way that his life is better today, then I can at this very moment still enjoy my share of that person's betterment, and that is a wonderful feeling.

Spiritual awakening can mean different things to different people. Among other things, spirituality means taking the focus off oneself and being more considerate of others. For the alcoholic or addict who recovers, the spirituality that comes with sobriety occurs when the self-centeredness of seeking only one's own contentment begins to be replaced by the greater consideration of others. As this consideration grows, one grows in spirituality. This can be just as valid as the person who never had an alcohol or drug problem.

The twelfth step is carefully worded: ". . . we tried to carry this *message*," and the corollary is "Carry the message, not the person." Our responsibility is to try to be of help to others, not to control them. The other person may not wish to listen to the message, and that is his prerogative. *Imposing* the message on others is not *carrying* it; in doing so, we overstep the boundary of genuine help and enter the area of co-dependence.

The application of the twelve steps to life as a whole is far broader than alcoholism, drug addiction, or other specific problems. One of the wonderful things about twelve-step programs is that they have a great deal of mutual devotion and unity. Recovering alcoholics, for example, know that they share one common enemy: alcohol. They know that they must stand together to triumph over this enemy and that their very lives depend on this triumph. They cannot afford to be divided. A recovering alcoholic knows that when asked to help someone, he must make himself available at any time of day or night.

Would it not be wonderful if everyone recognized that our triumph over the pitfalls of human frailty depended on our clinging together and being of help to each other? Would it not be a different world if we all realized that our individual happiness is contingent on the happiness of all?

Enter a room where there is an ongoing twelve-step meeting and look around. In attendance are rich and poor, highly educated and

illiterate, men, women, young, old, all races and creeds. Their individual differences and status in society were left outside, because within this room everyone is equal. Everyone is a human being, a person who is or has been in pain, and everyone is there for only one purpose: to get better by sharing. Twelve-step programs have implemented the message that has been taught for thousands of years: share with others. A sorrow that is shared is cut in half, a joy that is shared is doubled.

Whether the problem is alcohol or drugs or gambling or compulsive eating or whatever, one feature is found in all: loneliness. "No one understands and no one can help." Loneliness gives rise to anxiety and fear, the terrible fear of standing alone against overwhelming odds. The people in the twelve-step programs say "You are not alone because we are with you. We understand. There is no reason to be terrified, because together we can face even overwhelming challenges, and when we are together, the challenges cease to be overwhelming. Do not despair, because there is always hope. Just look around the room and you will see the reality of hope.

"If you would like what we have, then join us. No dues, no fees. Your contribution to the cause is being here, for no man is an island. You will help us, just as we will help you.

"Keep coming back. It works."

The term *spiritual awakening* is well chosen. A spiritual experience does not consist of the sky opening and a vision of celestial chariots amidst bolts of lightning and claps of thunder. It is an "awakening" because when one is asleep, one is not aware of what is going on right around him, and when he awakens, one's eyes are opened to see reality.

Too many people look for happiness elsewhere. There is nothing in their own lives which can give them happiness. If only things were different, if only they won the multimillion-dollar lottery jackpot. If only . . .

Happiness is not on the other side of the hill. There is just as much happiness available right where I am as elsewhere.

The climate may be more pleasant in other places. Delicacies may be more abundant elsewhere. The seashore provides fishing, swimming, surfing, and sunbathing. Other sections of town have affluent homes with spacious gardens.

Ask any psychiatrist. There are just as many troubled people in these desirable places as in any other.

On the other hand, there is just as much spirituality available right here as elsewhere. If my happiness is spiritual, I can find it right here.

Carrying the message does not consist of preaching. One of the traditions of the twelve-step programs is that they operate by attraction rather than promotion. "I am a person who has managed to escape from the clutches of this addiction, and my life is now so much better. If you wish to find out how I did it, I will be glad to share with you." There is no knocking on doors to attract new members.

Unfortunately, throughout the history of mankind, preaching has become suspect.

Too often in history the one who preached was dressed in warm clothes, and after saying a few empty, meaningless words, went on his way, leaving the sufferer out in the cold. Too often people talk too much and do too little.

To successfully carry the message, one must "practice these principles in all our affairs," because otherwise it is just preaching.

There are numerous idioms and aphorisms on the theme "Practice what you preach." So often we give lip service to very noble ideas, but our actions do not resemble our words in the least.

No thinking person can be at peace with himself if he is a hypocrite. The self-hatred that hypocrisy engenders may give rise to various defenses to conceal the duplicity. But alas! Even if we proclaim self-righteousness, we cannot deceive ourselves indefinitely.

The twelve steps are beautiful indeed, but only if we put them into action and practice them in all our affairs.

Some people seem to have a love affair with words. They make New Year's resolutions they know they will not keep, but the words sound nice anyway. They enjoy flattery even when they know it lacks sincerity. They are impressed by the promises of politicians even though experience has taught them that these are totally unreliable.

Spirituality requires honesty. If we have even the slightest aspiration to spirituality, we must progress beyond pleasant-sounding words and let our actions demonstrate the principles we espouse.

The twelfth is related to one of the program's traditions: If we wish to help someone overcome a destructive lifestyle, we do so by setting an example rather than by preaching.

Nothing is as powerful as a living example. Everyone is driven by the pursuit of happiness, and if we see someone living a lifestyle that is bringing him happiness we are likely to emulate him in order to gain happiness for ourselves. On the other hand, if a person is obviously not happy with the way he is living, no amount of preaching is going to convince us to adopt his lifestyle.

Charlie Brown means well, but Charlie is not the happiest of all persons—not by a long shot. Although we love Charlie and can often identify with him, the fact is that Charlie's poor self-esteem causes him much misery.

If Charlie Brown could see himself as the lovable person we know him to be and be content with himself instead of seeing himself as a failure, his feeling of self-esteem and contentment might well encourage others to emulate him.

It is only natural that, having discovered a new way of living that relieves us of so much misery and suffering, we would wish to share our good fortune with others.

It would be well to remember that when we were in the throes of our misery and someone suggested a way out, we were not exactly enthusiastically receptive. We were probably quite resistant in making any changes in ourselves. We should therefore be neither shocked nor offended when we bring the good tidings to others to

discover that they are not jumping with joy and do not shower us with their gratitude.

Nor should we be discouraged at being rebuffed. To begin, we may recall that although we too rejected recommendations others had made to us, we finally did come around to accepting a way out of our misery, and we are indeed appreciative of the efforts others made in our behalf.

Furthermore, every sincere effort to help does make some impact, even if this is not immediately apparent.

So don't be disappointed and don't be impatient. Good coffee takes time to perk.

Is it true that only a recovering alcoholic can help another alcoholic?

Not quite. There are many ways in which a person can be helped, and valuable counseling can come from knowledgeable persons who have not experienced a personal addiction. However, there are some aspects of alcoholism or other addictions that can never be fully understood by someone who has not shared the actual feelings of the addict.

There is nothing so terrifying as feeling that one is totally alone and that no one else can possibly understand how one feels.

A person who has survived any of the many hardships in life is a living testimony that there is life even after a severe crisis, and that there is hope even when everything appears bleak.

We are all survivors of one or another ordeal in life. We can

greatly contribute to relief of other people's distress if we share ourselves with others.

"I offered to help, and I was helped."

Some recovering alcoholics and drug addicts have said. "When I drank or used drugs I was selfish, and I have remained selfish even in my sobriety. What has changed about me is that I have turned myself in a direction to be helpful rather than harmful to others. When I try to help others to achieve sobriety, my own sobriety is reinforced."

How wonderful if we could all understand that whenever we help another person we receive much more than we give.

Charlie Brown is delighted to find a comrade, a finding that came about only as a result of his trying to help someone in distress.

Some wise man said that a joy that is shared is doubled, while a sorrow that is shared is halved.

Make it a practice to help others. You will be pleasantly surprised to discover who the real beneficiary is.

13

Co-dependence

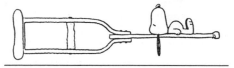

*R*ecently the twelve-step programs have placed emphasis on the phenomenon of *co-dependence*, a term that describes a relationship wherein you allow someone else to push your buttons. Rather than determining your own course in life, you react to another person's behavior, essentially allowing that person to manipulate your actions.

While this frequently happens in families where there has been an alcohol or drug addiction problem, it can occur in just about any

situation where you surrender your own thinking and your own de-cision-making to someone else. For example, some people are con-trolled by others who make them feel guilty if they do or fail to do something, and they therefore tailor their actions accordingly. Oth-ers are people-pleasers, always trying to satisfy someone else's wish-es instead of considering their own legitimate needs. In a way, the co-dependent looks at the world through someone else's eyes.

One of the features of the co-dependent relationship is that people in the environment of the person with problems often feel that they are the cause of the problems. Frequently the troubled person tries to lay a guilt trip on others and make them feel responsible for his difficulties—and too frequently they buy into this.

This is rarely valid. While my behavior may certainly place

stresses on people around me, how they choose to react to my behavior is their decision, not mine. The wife of the alcoholic frequently feels that she is at fault, that had she been a more devoted or capable wife her husband would not be drinking. Similarly, the spouses of the gambler, the overeater, the smoker, the workaholic all tend to assume responsibility for the problem, then react inappropriately because of their guilt.

Snoopy thinks that it was his licking that melted the snowman. He doesn't realize that he is not that powerful and that it was the sun that did it.

Maybe seeing ourselves as the cause of other people's problems gives us a weird feeling of power. We are so powerful that we can profoundly affect other people's behavior.

A bit of humility would help. There are countless other causes that result in problems, and we are rarely the primary cause.

We often hear it said: "No person is an island." True. But if we are all dependent on one another, then are we not all co-dependents? If

so, how can we talk about co-dependence as being a mal-adjustment?

There is a difference between interdependence and co-dependence. Of course no person can be an island. We are all dependent on one another in various ways.

In a healthy relationship, there is a fair exchange of dependence. No one is dominated and no one exacts a prohibitive price for the relationship.

Linus is paying an exorbitant price. If he is indeed dependent on Lucy for preparing his food, a sincere "Thank you" expressing his appreciation and gratitude should suffice. He should have no trouble in saying "Thank you," and a well-adjusted Lucy would have no need for anything more.

But as was pointed out in *When Do the Good Things Start?*, Lucy is domineering and Linus is co-dependent. The demands Lucy makes for her contribution to the relationship are unreasonable.

If you feel the demands of your partner are making you feel sick, you may be in a co-dependent relationship.

If you surrender the right to make your own decisions and allow others to run your life for you, you're really in trouble, because in order to change you have to make a decision that you are going to take over your own decision-making, and that decision may be overridden by whoever is making your decisions for you.

Is that too confusing? Maybe this illustration will clarify it.

Linus has allowed Lucy to dominate him. Linus is so intimidated by Lucy that she doesn't have to say anything to make him do something. She can control him with her silence.

Linus sends up a trial balloon that maybe he should not allow her to dominate him. Lucy dismisses this simply by ignoring the idea. Her message is that this is so totally absurd that it does not even require a response, so Linus promptly backs off.

Sound familiar?

It is important that one retain one's independence of thought and judgment. We should always listen to other people's opinions and give them careful consideration, but the ultimate decision should be our own.

If you think the world is cockeyed, you have the right to your own opinion, but don't assume the world to be cockeyed just because someone else believes it is.

If you keep your ears and mind open, listen to advice and to other people's opinions, and then process all the information and arrive at your own decision, you are likely to make a good adjustment to life. If you let yourself be manipulated by others, your life can really become confused. For example, what happens if you are subject to manipulation by two people whose opinions are divergent?

Poor Snoopy. He tries to satisfy everybody by keeping half his face sad and the other half cheerful. This may be impossible to do, and even if it is possible, it takes extraordinary effort to maintain two conflicting attitudes simultaneously.

But the major drawback is that after all the effort, Snoopy has really not satisfied anyone. Violet is dissatisfied with his cheerful half, and Patty is dissatisfied with his sad and droopy half.

So just be yourself and stop trying to satisfy everyone. Otherwise you'll wear yourself out and end up pleasing no one.

14

The Slogans

Easy Does It

*I*t is not always easy to keep one's cool, yet *easy* may be so essential to life that we have to be able to take it easy even when it is not easy to take things easy.

Think of how we react when we are provoked. Someone does or says something that irritates us. Our first impulse is to react. We may shout or sometimes utter an expletive.

Where does this get us? Nowhere! Whoever it was that provoked us is not in the least impressed. He still goes on believing whatever it was that he believed.

At this point Charlie Brown knows that nothing he says will change Lucy's mind, because that's the way Lucy is. So he wisely decides not to waste his energy trying to convince Lucy.

But then the urge to put Lucy in her place gets the better of him, and he decides to correct Lucy after all.

This just shows us why it is better to stick with "Easy does it" all the way. It might seem like putting the other person in his place is the thing to do, but when your first judgment was that it is of no use, stay with it. You are probably right.

One Day at a Time

*I*n a way, people might have had it easier when they had it harder.

Years ago, when things were really tough, people took it for granted that life was full of problems. Infant mortality was so high that it was an achievement to survive birth. Childhood diseases

were so common that it was an achievement to survive childhood. Tuberculosis was so widespread that it was difficult to make it to forty.

Today, modern scientific and medical miracles have pretty much made survival routine. We now have the luxury of being miserable with countless other things that our ancestors would have dismissed as trivia.

So Charlie Brown is discontented with the world.

Lucy tells him that reality may be unpleasant, but this is the only reality that exists, and he had better adjust to it.

Charlie Brown comes to the realization that coping with all of the difficult realities is more than any person can handle, but life *is* manageable if you break it into smaller pieces.

No point in dreading one's whole future. Just dread one day at a time.

*I*nasmuch as our energies are not infinite, it makes good sense to use them sparingly. Wasting energy on something futile is not only unwise, it is also exhausting, frustrating, and depressing.

Think about what you can do today. If you can put away some of your pay and savings so that you can afford a vacation in the summer or perhaps in a pension plan for when you retire, that is perfectly appropriate. There is nothing wrong with planning ahead and providing for the future. But to sit and worry today about something that may occur in the future *that you can do nothing about* is wasteful and frustrating.

This is what is meant by "Take one day at a time."

In addition to avoiding unnecessary and unconstructive worry, the "One day at a time" slogan also suggests doing today what one should do today and not procrastinating. How much grief we could spare ourselves if we could overcome procrastination!

The book will not have any fewer pages tomorrow. And the task will be the same and there will be less time in which to get it completed.

People in the environment of the procrastinator may actually encourage procrastination and then criticize the person for it. . .

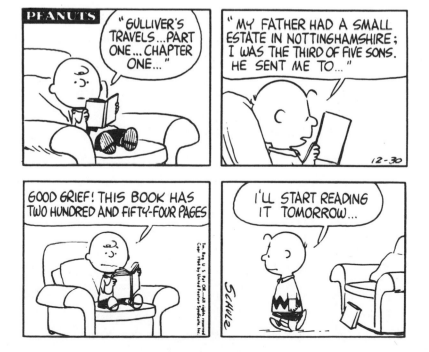

Or nag him . . .

Or just be silent . . .

The results of procrastination are universally bad. We wear ourselves to a frazzle in the panic of the final moments.

And the final product testifies to our procrastination . . .

First Things First

Many problems arise as a result of failure to set priorities. We may desire many things, but if reality dictates that we cannot have them all, then we must make choices.

Most people must be on a budget. As desirable as diamonds, vacations, and outboard motors may be, food, clothing, shelter, and health care must come first. If we must limit our calories, essential nutrients must take priority over candy. If a ball game and an important business meeting conflict, the meeting should take priority.

Why is this so? Why can't we have everything that we want? Who dictated that food must come before an outboard motor? Well, no one really ever put the issue to a vote.

Why are some children older than others? Because they were born first. Is that completely fair to the younger child who did not have a say in the matter? Maybe not, but that is reality.

An acceptance of reality the way it is rather than the way we like it to be is essential for a healthy adjustment to life.

Live and Let Live

Live and let live is a wonderful principle. If no one is encroaching on your territory, don't interfere with their lifestyle. Live the way you wish, and allow others to live the way they wish.

How much suffering and misery could be avoided if we only followed this simple rule. Other people do not have to do things the way I do, nor do they have to believe the way I believe. If everyone respects everyone else, people can live together peacefully.

Since this principle is so simple and elementary, why is it not observed and followed more frequently?

We give lip service to other people's basic rights, but in the very same breath we say that what they are doing isn't right at all, so it is not protected by our respecting their basic *rights*.

This is a very flimsy rationalization for our wish to dominate other people or, at the very least, coerce them to accept our values.

If we took the "Live and let live" motto literally and without rationalizations, we would all be much happier.

Time Takes Time

In spite of modern technological miracles such as the microwave oven and the fax machine, there are some things that simply cannot be hurried, like pregnancy.

Similarly, changes in one's personality or emotional makeup

cannot be hurried. Some people look to hypnosis as a quick fix, which it isn't. Others go for various pills in the hope that they will feel better instantaneously. Unfortunately, looking for a quick fix emotionally often leads to dependence on chemicals and addiction.

On the other hand, some people go to therapists forever and may delay making necessary changes in their lives in the hope that the therapist will find an easier way in which they can feel better while they continue to do whatever it is they have been doing until now.

Waiting for short periods of time is reasonable. If it looks like it is going to take twenty years, it would appear more advisable to make some changes in the team than to expect the team to improve.

Keep It Simple

Simple problems often can be resolved by simple solutions. Many problems in life could be resolved fairly simply if only we kept them simple. Too often we muddy the waters and turn simple problems into very complex ones.

Why?

In all likelihood, Sally did not get her dad anything for Father's Day, and because she is reluctant to admit it she confuses the question and leads Charlie Brown on a wild goose chase.

This is a favorite ploy of politicians who refuse to answer a question when the answer would be embarrassing to them.

When we complicate things that are really quite simple, it is invariably because the simple solution or answer is not to our liking.

Think, Think, Think

Sometimes too much thinking can get one into trouble. In fact, the slogan "Keep it simple" is a warning to avoid complicating simple things by too much thinking.

There are, however, many times when a bit of thought could stop us from doing something foolish. How often have we reflected on something we did or said and realized "How silly that was. Why did

I do (or say) something so stupid?" Such embarrassing situations could be avoided if we just gave some forethought to what we do or say.

The fact that the comic strips use *woof* to indicate the bark of a dog does not mean that dogs say "woof." Nor do birds say "cheep" or angry cats say "rowr." We must appear quite silly to animals if we try to communicate with them in this manner. Why, then, do we do so? Because we don't think about what we are saying.

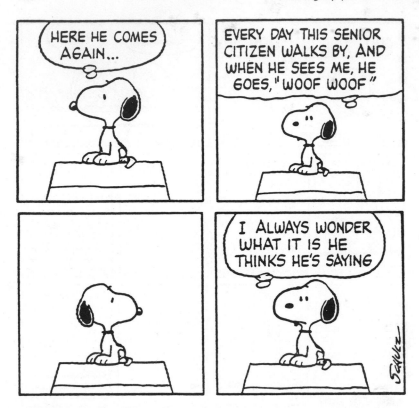

No great harm is done in saying something meaningless to an animal. It is quite different when we say something to other people without first thinking if we are making any sense. At best, thoughtless speech may be foolish, but at worst, it can also be insulting or painful.

In this respect, it is good to think, think, think.

Postscript

In Gateway Rehabilitation Center there is a sign: "The Elevator to Recovery Is Out of Order. Please Use the Twelve Steps." Improving one's personality is not an easy ride. One must make the effort to climb.

Although the Twelve Steps are not an elevator, they do bear a similarity to an escalator. The latter is a continuous chain, where eventually the uppermost step circulates and becomes the first step again.

Ideally, personality development never ceases. At any one time a personal analysis may reveal parts of our character that require improvement, and we can then go about correcting those defects. However, once we have refined our character we may notice new items that bear correction that we had not previously considered to be shortcomings, but that now appear to be incompatible with the new personality that has emerged.

It is similar to redecorating your living room. Now that you have beautiful new furniture, you find that the old carpet clashes with the decor, and you therefore need a new carpet. The new carpet shows up the drabness of the wallpaper, and so that must be replaced. But the beauty of the room cannot be appreciated because of the inadequate lighting, so you must buy new lamps. Each improvement necessitates another improvement.

The Twelve Steps are a superb guide to personality development, but they are indeed an escalator. Once you have reached the twelfth step, you cannot step onto a platform and declare, "I have arrived!" Rather, from your new vantage point you reexamine yourself and find that there are facets of your character that are incongruous with your new personality, and so you begin the chain of improvement once again. No finer philosophy of life has ever been proposed.

Sometimes we sleep away our lives, going through the motions of living much like a sleepwalker. Occasionally something stimulates us to examine whether we really are all that we want to be or all that we can be. This arousal is the first step, an awareness that we have been oblivious of ourselves. We can then resolve to do whatever it takes to become everything we are capable of becoming.

This is "Waking Up Just In Time."